Backup to

Backup to Babylon

Poems, 1972–1987

MAXINE GADD

Vancouver

NEW STAR BOOKS

2006

NEW STAR BOOKS LTD.
107 – 3477 Commercial Street
Vancouver, BC V5N 4E8   CANADA

1517 – 1574 Gulf Road
Point Roberts, WA 98281   USA

www.NewStarBooks.com
info@NewStarBooks.com

Publication of this work is made possible by grants from the
Canada Council, the Department of Canadian Heritage, the
Province of British Columbia, and the British Columbia Arts
Council.

Photo on frontispiece by Elaine Brière
Cover by Mutasis Design
Printed and bound in Canada
by Imprimerie Gauvin
Printed on chlorine-free,
100% post-consumer recyled paper
First printing, July 2006

LIBRARY AND ARCHIVES CANADA
CATALOGUING IN PUBLICATION

Gadd, Maxine
    Backup to Babylon / Maxine Gadd.

Poems.
ISBN 1-55420-024-5

    1. Downtown-Eastside (Vancouver, B.C.) —
Poetry. 2. Vancouver (B.C.) — Poetry. I. Title.

PS8513.A22B32 2006   C811'.54   C2006-900553-2

contents

greenstone

cabin on the shore

backup to babylon

greenstone

in the backwoods

across rainy Georgia Strait from dominatrix city on an island amongst islands known for thousands of years, a two hours walk on small settled roads to the beginning of a forest under a green mountain cradling a dark green cove, an old orchard and meadow sloping northwest, a run down yellow house, many collapsing outhouses, tool sheds, wood sheds, chicken coops, garages carpeted about with exquisitely disintegrating components of antique internal combustion motors: springs and levers, axles separated from wheels, bolts, wires, nails, blades rusting into the colour of the cedar bark browze

back of all that, a cabin with a woodpile, axes, wedges, mauls, saws, black nights, fire, silence, soft cries of owls and wounded deer, fire, and neighbours' tales

utopia

this fire now
as familiar
as Jesus
an ancient mystery
i can tell the story
pull the coals forward
leave a throat
for the draught
of air

be comforted

beware

Old Joe

you remember Old Joe, the handyman, helped out on the farm, burned
down the house, made us all sit out in the fields and forests and on the
beaches under the stars
Old Joe
once the husband of Mary, the luminous mystery strange paleface Joe,
you think maybe he is crazy? where is Joe now that we don't
see him any more? hanging out in the backwoods or listening at the door?

be careful of yr baby on days of high wind

there is this struggle we were having on the dirt floor of our cabin
was it the distraction of animals, hollow voices of the world over water
against the simple *immanence* of the numinous, the "divine nod"?

> how you can awaken only in that dream
> that sort of sleeping
> forbidden by the forty hour tyrants of time

the glitch is
the several hundred bikers roaring onto the yellow grass plain
under the rise our tents were on
one summer
somewhere beyond Edgewood

> me a little blue gnome mum
> shivering in my tent with my
> child and my pen then
> jumping up and down with
> my little blue axe

cancel all that

start again where it
began
would you
make
more
massacre
of Bessarabia or
Illyricum

would you walk in the city of gardens
      yr face fall open
            to the ivory gods
                  under the windless blue
full of ancient denials
            a thousand years

                           and now
                           the wind

         metropolis of ruin
         mistress of time
         there are no taxis

to take me racing fast past gaping stone mansions wanting to swallow me
   whole in their lonely stone mouths

                         i must stop
                         i must go
                         i must stop
                         i must go

         now
         now
         now

                              down the mountain
                                  where he waits
                              my neapolitan guide
                                  an ancient drunk
                              with amethyst nose
                                      now
                              blue with fury
                                  then
                              yellow with fear

for we have held up the great ship for me
and the power of dead Pompeii

79 BC

eyes ^{are} *eyes* ^{are}

                           are   are
                    eyes   eyes

i go back to being
           Maxine (i was going to say
"that selfish person") and because
      in the rain and the fishboat out there
        clams and
the cabin is warmer now

all the old stories are gone
even Theseus the kindly woodchopper

           all the old stories are
        lined up with my books, sitting there
              amber-eyed
            like dæmons
                 all the old stories
          counter-point
        to what i've encountered
    and am compelled to recount
        two women sit in the wilderness
            tracing their various descents
               off the racial goddesses

is theirs envy or only a wild delight in the tale?
all the blue feathers of the peacock and the white of the dove and the grey
         and the black of the crow and the raven
            the crown of the hair of a queen
    or any Armenian in sunlight
now it's forbidden, race
            the sweet dark and light of eyes
                black, grey, green, brown and blue
                multitudinous jewels

you went to her out of duty
you went to her out of fear
you went to her out of terror
you went to her out of love

the highway was yellow
the barns cowered in the bed-like fields
the houses were all under storm,
down through holes
the blue sky rolled

i remembered a day when i could pray for prairies when i met the golden
    mountains all around
ground devils, cute as gophers came up
and Satan's Angels roaring through the peaceful dream / The Prince
    never came to Nakusp
I didn't write him a letter

how else can come the blue green goddess of the southwest
the silver blue goddess of the northwest
                how can the purple goddess of the northeast
                    and the yellow goddess of the southeast
how can the emerald goddess of the east
        and the coral goddess of the west
how can the black goddess of the north and the red goddess of the south
how can the goddesses of fire and water and earth and air how can the
goddesses of matrimony and fertility and lust and imagination, how the
goddesses of knowledge and wisdom and science and art
                how can the goddesses of Job
                    Daniel and Deborah
                        and Miryam
                        and Joan

        how can they, how can they, how can they?

the hunter

the hunter walks in the sun, the hunter misses the sun, whoever made sorrow yr lover? visit the sands of Egypt. don't

step into Cinderella's shoes. get yr sweet boy on the road, on the sea, be as free of him as the hunter is of the deer.

the doctor

for George Heyman
and Scott Lawrence

this has to be all to the New Family which is those that want it
i have set myself up as Doctor
come and be cured in the space and time that I alone prescribe
set apart a time in the day no one will come to disturb
no child crying
no old man who is dying
no young man in pain
no woman who has troubles
no purposively addicted animal
needing to be fed not even yr own self needing a pile of wood

forget your concern for and need for
the complex and expanded world
its surrealisms and cartwheels and
catherine wheels and monkeys and monks
do not care
what comes sweeping in on the pacific ocean
fail brothers and sisters and fathers and cousins
be well looked after by mothers and daughters
sweltered

let angels attend you
always
those angels

chickens and raccoons
            falling off the cedar trees

purposes
of persons
prowling
for still space in the calm rain and healthy
water table

reincarnations extending to stars only mental in the laboratory
till their eyes are twisted
by something in structure
the pain of revelation and of news

backwards

every day yu slide a little backwards into the woodpile that shrinks into
　　the hungry void.
face it; it aches. if you never leave yr home you'll never have to go home
　　alone.
it is necessary to see the cobwebs grow and the white chickens on the hill
are an industry pacific supreme salmon-line lies about with white wool
what a superwoman can't do
when she puts her mind to *it*

turn the fire down, turn the light bulb out, *it's* hunting, *it's* howling.

a black cat with golden eyes is following, is saying it's not quite that way.
surrendering the prospect of fame and cancer, or just a waste of time in
elevators i retreat into the distant little kingdom of sensibility, artful dirt,
　　low cedar light,
raven note, a bell on clean sea, the tide out,
birds searching the soul of sand, the eight foot diameter clam lying three
　　feet below
the surface.

this desperation for products produces in literature, wit,
which is the soul of brevity, the clam in the sand, the scholar in her
　　library,
stringing out a bit of grit for her city, eventually the pearl of great price to
　　hang
round the neck
of a slave.

the woods-dreamers' children, weary of peace will seek that pearl.

fr Beth and Don Juan and their yacky ways

               wld yu like that dream in the tree?
or pale hands wandering all over yr body crying for yr power
               easy to be a dæmon lover on twenty thousand a year
black as the kabaala he turned west at the tip of Finland
went down in the whirlpool chanting the fifty million names of god

it did him no good
now yu can read about him in the *New Yorker* in yr warm bed with
buttered crumbs

examine yr own torn hands and enter the wounds
meet the amber-eyed spider inside yu
yu find it goes in for personal growth
wld jog on Davie st. if the police wld leave it alone

               it has a marvellous memory of witches
               the holy ones
squeaks anxiously of their dreams
                   their transmogrifications
                 into the north and south poles
it sez
we shld set out laughing if we set out at all
ladies' limbs are shaking off the blood of baby seals
ladies' hands are setting out the loaves and fishes
                  their lover brings
                  gallons of wine

when the mountain cracks asunder we'll greet the same old grief
we'll turn on the sixty minute little wheel
reeling in second hand jeans for our raving children

meet me under the clothes line we'll do some smoke
plan to be president of the union of cement mixers, write a course on how

to die like an eagle
(eating an arsenic-soaked corpse, of course)

shore up *petite-bourgeoises*!

printers and painters and poets how
will we ever fly like farmers?

suburb

They
are all leaving me in a mass and a rush from the bus.
what a relief
after I made myself responsible for all those eyes
                                        all those I's.

Condoms

                                        cast

in the centre
of the great

                              ring

of the the freeway winding round
all those dreams
                                        all those dreams.

                        She
                        sits
knitting every thought
into a garment
to shield her against
the future wind

                        flash of agony
                        flash of joy
                        shopping lists
                        relationships
                        birthdays
                        shovelsful of clay
                        every nail
                        illuminated
                        with the accumulated
                        experience
                        of billions
                        of builders.

Behind
the trees
houses
shimmer
dangerous
as radium.

not talking about Spender's gazelle

not talking about Spender's gazelle nor the dummy
        you have agreed to die into
talking about the small, neatly drunk poet about to die in the snow
        at solstice or February when the stars are still mean talking
        about
the Game, which seems good at the time
        the Game that the righteous camper plays with its new
        lover, Nature
before heading back to the post at BC Hydro

movement

the richness drowns you
relationships that you have run from
then sobbed
alone
for the million
empty
rooms

who is serious, who is gay, who cuts up lovers, who wanders to Calgary
who makes a farm work, keeps the horses from coughing and colic, who
sings in the wilderness?

the stars shine pink and silver on the telly. kidnappings, murders fill
    someone

spiders also
incite to communication

is there, after all an intricate meaning to the pattern of persons who
    wander this city this night?

what could the pattern signify if not me?

and who is this who right now
should be going out?

is my life in this ruby, co-ordinates of leaf patterns and rachael stitch
the effects planned
or the hysterical friend?

one sends a letter

sorry, our illusions could not
coincide
except with such a will
as neither of us can comprehend

sometimes
friends
sometimes
lice

courage is lost

who is this that sends herself on a mission?
what does she come for?
why is she here?

colour cuts out the army enters
one decides to not exercise ones will

someone cuts out
goes to the mountains

madre, the king
explodes a space where the cowboys bow

who cares
the seeresses are in jail?

the seeresses
emerge from my left and right hemispheres, they are lizards or
small army tanks the size of my fists.

can they meet the morning or are they to die drunk?

what society
will feed them
the belief
they need?

the admission charge to the city

is yr love, yr willingness
to be in the myth:
it hardly matters that yu fail; it keeps you
in the streets,
it hardly matters that you die,
yr myth congeals,
it hardly matters that you love
it hardly
matters.

in the country the city is thinned out and loses itself and slumjungle
monsterman has a fishboat and marries his mother; yr love meets the
speculation of a spider and shrinks to worm

and now there's time to wonder what there was
                              in the city

in the wilderness yu meet the spirit standing transparent and luminous
directly before you on your path; it says, "Come,
I will be everything to you."
but you will wander in and out for years of your life
driven by Love, which is a propeller-driven aeroplane
landing in paradise, always with instructions to return
               instructions to return
to Space Mother
who does not forget her messengers and demands at cost of yr horror
    what all humans will demand,
the use of yr power with no commitment to return it to you
a slumdrunk will bring yu to his room on Hastings East and you will see
flocks of Aphrodite's birds beat up from the golden bowery
shamans
on the stairs will give yu pantherina and amanita muscaria.

In a cosmic roar, with lightning spasms blinding yu
yu
will find yrself hollering a dozen people laughing
and yu all ripped casting off from the Fraser river in a fishboat
                    into the
strait.

my 135th feminist nightmare

what a to-do / here's a chinook wind, dec.15 / going north northwest
      with the fire blue dog of poetry
            everyone
                      getting along so friendly
so very friendly
tra la laa little lizard queens slanty-eyed, smiling
always smiling, québecoise girlwives, cheerful, resourceful,
italian mamas singing calabrian imprecations
yiddisher mamas distributing snacks
brisk brusque british academic spinsters, jolly faced, funny,
sunny southern belle dingalings, punjabi houris, hula gals,
skinny help mates from the heartlands of the boney west,
              snickery
        school girls drilling with the auger
        so the whole boat sinks

        everybody's drowning
tall black athletes skim across the ocean and outofsight
elegant debutantes swooped up by hydroplanes
chubby little mothers of all colours going under, all ballooning orange
calico skirts, babies bobbing about, crazed mothers releasing them quickly
from all bonds of clothing, loving couples strangling each other in the
   briney foam

           some cats swim
           some cats drown
      long haired dogs paddle about laughing
           laughing
what lettuce to eat on the rice? what perpendicular rat holes entrance
you on into the mystery of personality, what types on Mars are
        up to, on

Aldebaran
on
Analgest
?

pick up yr package yesterday
or it's gone gone gone ...
same with yrself and yr tiny elephantine joys.
do them.
do them now.
do them
before now.

the tide is going out and with it the world's supply of wheat
it's that gift of italian light i begged her for
the pale blue angels
peering into my eyes
so that the terror
is made and laid

****
my m-cat blazes back at me her topaz fire
* *
*
****

deep in the ice palace the light is boundless
walking fast yu smash into invisible walls
parades of amazons and barbarians
manifesting and dissolving
slow dimming
of diamond white
to moon white
to water waver
to dusk and darkness, horror dawning, do you remember black

26

yu are dying in the hollow cold, fingers freezing, knees, wrists, feet
disappearing

the night stars shrieking
radium axe crash
and the silvery stranger wafts his cloak into a steel–like tunnel
up through ice
to air
that tears
like *eagles claws that rip yr eyes*
yr own blood fills yr throat
yu fight
the steel hook
til yu agree
to fall apart
pincers seize yr arm
yu
go
limp

are
let
drag
till the steel teeth of the sea make yu scream

a grey faced policeman
hauls yu up
"easy there; everything will be all right"

yu are thrown to the floor of the Zodiac and

thump
thump
thump

the little mums
come tumbling after

(some are down with broken crown)
and we are speeding towards the mother ships
and stop
at the gullet
of some hideous
new city

i am held tight
shivering
convulsively

an argument
in esperanto
continues
endlessly

      i bury my head under an army blanket thrown over my body
                                   but look up
                         for azure mantelled Chinook
            she is gone
            into the grey

            ice
            comes on
i will sell my soul   for warm hands

oriental medicine (Tang Kwei Gin)

a bright liquid to be
"taken with water"
or whatever
we have to
to "get it together"
bunched up
as we are
inexorably tangled
some of us "a little wilted"

and some
burgeoning
golden
dæmons

a buncha the gals was whoopin it up in
Crazy Jane's Saloon

up comes the judge and sez git
back to yr typing
up yors, yr honor sez Olga
glow worm
staring
down
an abyss
that sinks
for a mile

and yes by the A Allah
a pale green plain extending to the azimuth where the mild and woolly
wild young clouds gather radiant with liberation

well she sed i don't
have to stick this

and leapt, thoroughly enjoying the prospect all the way down
     till she hit the parapet

      and then the black the red the black the red the
black the red the black the red the black the red the black the red the
black the red the black the red the
black the red

        and there she was again
          back in the pub

"extract of white flowered peony can oppress the convulsion of the
verticle muscles of the abdomen or the other muscles and can have the
centre of the nerves enfeebled. It is, therefore, effective for the treatment
of postpartum hæmorrhage, stomach ache
lumbago
menorrhagia
and reversal menstruation"

menorrhea
rhea
river
dream mother who flows

that you might begin as the bud of a white rose, and as spring becomes
summer and the urge of the itch to begin

      till the burst bomb of the bloom
and a lion appears in the garden
   that leaps
    to yr throat
     and yu swoon
     crying on Christ and all the dæmons mob you
      mocking you, flaming

entrancing and drawing yu
flying with yr sacred
ordinary body thru the
skies to meet " 'Saint
Peter at the gate

and what
does he ask those golden boddhisattvas, hand in hand with the pale blue
saints of abnegation and *endless* serenity?

'what have you done on this earth!' "

black flag

white paper
between me and the dream of union
the word to protract
direct action

sagging typewriter ribbon
running between the reels like a drunk's black banner
the poet's banner / the philosopher's banner / banner of
bandleaders alone in a crowd
the crowd's black banner
the banner of all those not carrying

a	a	a	a
red	green	blue	white
flag	flag	flag	flag

"flag", a turf, a sod, a flake, a crack, a *flaw*
flaga, flawe
a flake, a breach, a crack
in the *crowd*

this way
follow me
to a certain death
and a well-greased press

"creoden" crouden, "to crowd, to press, to push hard"

make up yr mind
whether to follow the black
flag, each
rag
a piece of the poet's banner, the philosopher's banner all torn up and
distributed widely

                    bed room banner
                    bar room banner
                    the banner no one prints
the unthinkable
        the unsayable
                utterance of
                        the exclusively
                            human
                                    emotion
                                            despair

place of the first true kindness
place where we say

                                    it's no good
                                    it won't work
                                what's the use
                            but we are moving
                                mass–mate
                                be my eyes
                                be my ears
                            leave me a space
maybe as much as

                                    an atom
                                    spins
                                    in

Maxine meets Proteus in Gastown

scene 1

1967, the street

Cordova
has led me lonely
from the mountain pass
all night long
the Indians are singing carry me away red eyed dæmons
rush past me and my friend
hunkering in the little hatchway filled with bliss
filled with the young one's dream
of midnight living
of giant blue souls
of the noble nine foot monk
striding thru
this mountain highway
　　　　his huge hand field up *halt*
　　　　　　the hand of my friend Martin
the little rat faces holding hard
　　　　to our stories for five year olds

Dr. Fu Manchu squats
down beside us and invites us home
for a drink
with the Dalai Lama
It is hard to refuse
such finesse
but we want to wait
till this
street

is gold
at dawn
my friend
has disappeared

and for half an hour the wind takes me down to the

trees
where an old man
is twisting the body
of a rat

he looks at me sadly and sez
i cn show you where the bears are but
they
they're too big fr me now
and the farmers shoot yu if yu even ask

fr a job and fr welfare
yv got to have an address at the Hung Up Inn
where the young junkies wld twist my body like this rat's

so yu cn devour this with some equanimity, say i conferring on
the old man a robe of red velvet come on across the water, he sez and see
    where i live
tis the ancient forest, i come into town for the kill the kill only

and what of yr friends say i
wondering of mine

heroes, ma'am, he sez, all brave like yrself and tight, tight
as an arse that speaks; they despise all that's ignoble like myself
but you, you oh lady they'd take to the highest estate, come
meet the princes of the forest

and amazons there are there too all thrust into life
shining with inheritance
though none will spend a sou
for the soul of old Jean Paul

yr from Mallardville, then, are yu, i ask
unstitching the soles of the old man's shoes
yr fever's past, buddy
these now go to the soup
for the one last union

ah, Pegasus, he cries
yu cldn't spare an hour to take an old man to Dairyland

my pleasure, say i
maybe they'll let you keep yr rat in their fridge
and we walk off, hand in hand

coming up powell street into the rising sun
me feeling soft and gentle as an old lady who has done no wrong
who gave birth to children like butter
                    and kept them alive in apple trees
            who took them all swimming in the one big sea
                    and now has been set free
                        to enter her city

scene 2

so we trip up the marble stairs of the People's Liberation Palace
and enter a dim mysterious hall with pillars of white stone just
standing around
where's the washroom i ask the princess
                    there, she sez, rather annoyed. i notice
                              yu didn't ask
                              The President

      no use arguing, i had to get in and see just how old
i was.
a young lady, fat and beautiful coming out of the cubicle
      sez, hi, yu want to come to a party?
i couldn't see why not
but i didn't have any money and as far as i cared to look
I was suffering from
                        total amnesia; well
                          yll have to keep
                    yrself better she sez
           with a snoot and a sweep
from the hall

              i looked left and right
                    was safely alone
                          and went to the mirror
              there to be shown
yes, a very bad tempered
              79 yr old — naw, maybe 62
      with looks like this i cld really go far
but not to the bar   the bench maybe
      or the right wing of city hall but my head waz not ready
(fair's fair)
      so how to get back to fair forty two?

scene 3: the ancient princess enters Woodward's food floor

        this is not Hades, dark as it seems to the lover of the sun
this is the court of the ten o'clock cup of tea
this is the place to meet
      not spare the dollar

all for old
bones
old
bones

this is how we might
spend the day together

this is the tropic garden, this is where they mix

the nuts
                and here am i in hibiscus, my own gran dam
wonder who got my rat
yr not
sittin there daddering, my deer, my only
      daughter   she's
kaing of the partenons
        o surely, and the best of it all to

you
kin i wake a talon fr yu? and surely, me hee hee hee
          tin of soup a day
my daughters won't let me starve

and here comes those queee boys pace yrself, Marcie, yr true
world's a coming
that nightmare

it was knitted in Hollywood, some
big fat general thinks he's the Queen, takes a bomb or two
off the bottom of the blue

kow tow! kow tow! kow tow!
                    seoul sole soul sol so
                              she
                         kiss, he sed
                         and i
                              did
so he's so sweet you know, and she too
yu know, pal, i got the best damn scheme for you today, and won't
you regret it Monday
if yu don't take the best damn soul
          searching and   then
the treasure   the treasure
          i know where it is, up on that mountain pass there
among the wandering detectives
they've got this flying platform, yu know

they never miss

Bobby, come out here and wheel the cart!
          whirr, whirr, she see, whiirr whiirr and then babby come out here
and meal the horse,
               honey, come out and play the course

                         whirr whirr he sez and then
Bobby come out here and place it all
               place it all away or
               here
                              Bobby
                         make it all white
                              all right?

39

into dead space she fell
and never knew any better, if yu know what i mean
yull never get out

                                    and now yu know
                                        now yu know

this is Old Town
Old Town

but i'm fed up with it all i sed to the food floor, with twenty million years
of feeding and eating. i'm tired of the ironic big complaint and the smile
of the ill clutching at yu into their sweetness
and i myself cld be ill very very ill   again   and   again
the beatitude of the powerful
                        how kind i am not to kill yu
so here am i
so deep into the information that any hummingbird can ignore

ay, i'm fed up with it too but how will we do without our daily murder,
some big mouthed scum get too mouthy, they say they come down in a
helicopter took him away some buddy and their tyranny and what's that
but a personal endorsement, something fairly long in the line, with a head
and a tail, full of paddles and handles and dorsal fins from the over long
line that unites yr need for horror and the last warm fire on earth?

        skill fr them, all me dears, i keep on wanting to upset yr
shopping basket.
                    what about me? all this time i'm being avoided
                    when the *old* time story told me
                            that i
                        and i alone
            wld be queen of the woods and all the nymphs and heroes
                        join me at play

toot toot toot little mistress, yv all the young rockers to look at
now. the old man who's a hero's made a fool in a chair

all this excellent chinaware   biscuit finish better'n skin ormolu

who's that, some opera singin gorilla?

                    fancy
how yu cn stab an old woman in the back in plain sight of
all her fans

(the blue god enters and speaks:)

ffffffffffffffff
f
f
f
fff
fane
fan
fanatic
fanum
fane
fan
fanatic fanum fane
fan fan fan fan fan fan fan fan fan fan fantastic
fanum
holy
temple

and all that's before
pro
fane

or for it
the wind
in the sack at the end of the sock
sez the gaffer
hand me a hoochie, honey
we gonna get down there

under the tide

scene 4: Hastings and Main

the dark eyed Dene boy
he stop yu on
the street

he
say
hey, where yu going
and i
say
yu can't stop me
yu got no right

he laughs
he steps back
he say
okay
let's see
some ID, then

i turn up my nose like Pretty Pepperidge Meggy
who sells sweet and nutty pies frum the farm
frum the freezer

no use
looking back

no problem
who i
am
on this
day

cabin on the shore

the cabin on the shore

one of six shanties, ten foot by twelve foot and ten foot tall supported
in the back on rusting oil drums standing in a creek running behind an
ancient shell midden that is gradually being destroyed by the huge soft
suckings and violent lashings of thousands of years of tides that twice
every twenty four hours leave human messages of burnt clam shells, layers
of ash, neat little black arrow heads, part of a ceremonial green jade axe

by day the sea vacates ten acres of emerald green moss or provides the
sleeper upon awakening with a baroque hall of vastly impossible gleaming
floors and strange courtiers, the yachts: by August, a city on the sea, by
fall, all gone like a raid of butterflies

and the migrating ducks come back and settle chuckling near the shore,
the herons resume their meditations knee deep in the significant fish and
a piece of a prow of a old boat once painted white with a Phoenician eye
drifts with the ebb and the flood and the ebb and the flood in the limits of
the cove

one day it disappears forever

perception

                                    person
                                    pursued
                                    by
                                    pumas

bird

        floating

              on

                      common

sense

                                    human
                                    humanizes
                                    sysssss
                                    tematically

permit me
clarity
twisted
window

                                    a boat
                                    in the Gobi
                                    desert
                                    painted blue

won't
      you
            come
                  running
                        running
                              running

that
red and blue
moth
on
th
i
n
n
n
s
t
r
i
n
g

the wreck of the good ship Sisyphus

nameless
boat
sailing
into the rain
away
from shame
the shape
trig
to
go where the world's breathing
sends me

to the formal
edge
of another
lie
the rock
face
of an unfamiliar shore
or the photograph
in the newspaper

the boat not paid for
he fled to wild islands

a good sailor
must be crazy
to have learned all that

more news for the plastic rainbow tribe

Charlie's dark eye headed south
i'm not twenty
would go with great care now
take two loads of forty pounds
think about carrying the cats
have a red lacquered box with a glass
discuss
the two large dome tents we would buy

the sea at Galiano Bali blue
troubling me with travelling mountains
they are waves
stay out of their way

i take on the blue man of my mind
he kills me with cold
in January i open and close doors
try to make heat
take a slender round file
sharpen my heart

food

i have to try to live in it the thing where the food is that i think so
    beautiful

now it looks
               like a huge sheet of steel
                    and it's coming toward me

                              it is the mistress covered
                              with sharks in little styrofoam ships

                                      they celebrate
                                      freedom with
                                      Portuguese wine and
                                      call the vintner a
                                      cunt

cabin

start over again don't accuse yr neighbour unfairly nor bear
false witness
lie like socks
must be knit
for cold
feet

potlatch
chinook
Cowichan
Halkomen

in the 1920s newspaper
"O Chew Wan
this renegade native"
who lived in a cave across the cove

"not bad,"
he said before they hanged him, "twelve white man for one Injun"

firelion

firelion
leaps
thru the window
butts
my elbow
makes
muddy pawprints
all over this page

light the lamp stoke the stove simmer the rice

looking for last night's salty singer
no nightingale
only
a gull
at dawn
tells me of the coast
a slope
that never eases

Nicaragua
        Peru
               Chile
                      Salvador

it was a bluegrey corridor of cloud

struggle of flying thru white bushes
                              also a conception
                hard to keep the way
                                              wass ist der   ?
                        this is the

                                                      jet roar
                                                      to the north

                                                      up that
                                                      coast
                                        ceaseless screams

                        Comox
                                        this intrusion
                                        in my dream

sailing to San Salvador

do you believe
in the good
wind
the water from heaven
sharks and turtles
struggle aboard
for yr soup

flying to San Salvador

500 miles to Crescent City
  600 miles to Banta Barbara
    400 miles to Rosario
      500 miles Topolobampo
        400 miles Tuxpan
          400 miles Popocatapetl
            400 miles Juchila
              400 miles San Salvador

the contralmirante answers

Si.
Well, Senorita, I tell you at least you send me a polite and (fairly) clean
    letter begging me for these lives.
I do
take life seriously
as mine has been taken
bit by bit
daily
all these years

Well, yes,
beating?
they used to make you drink your own blood.
life was not easy, then, madam, even for a white.

My reasons?

Go and ask General Ibañez de Tilleria.

Ask him
about Margarita Sepulveda

What does it matter, madam,
who I
am?

What can it matter?

out of sync

off base\
not in tune

riotous, selfish, unruly

a wooly herd of buffalo named:

An-Bang Aaron Aline Bachir Badriyah Bo-Lan Calder Cadogan Clliiig-
Ling Dagmar Dabert Da Wei Eamon Ebba Eve Fadoul Ferola Fen-Ding
Galen Gui-Cl-iun Gerry Eamon Evelyn Gay Helen Hagos Haldis Inali
Isra Issa Jorens Jagoda Ja-Ni Kamall Kishi Kun-Lan Lysander Lubmilla
Louise Maso Mako Manny Ngwe-Khaing Nildag Nao-Mi Orban Ottillia
Du-Bei Po-Mya Pellkita Pi-Le Quinlan Quenby Kwa-nuen Raihanna
Ronald Ruo-Fu Svenborn Selvaggia Shan-Li Taddea Tayanita Te-Lao
Ullric Urano U-Bei Vivien Vev-@Lna Vinnie Vaughn Wilford Wanda
Wik-To-Ya X4-Men Xylia Xavier Yitzhak Yu-Jun Yehudi Yuell Zale Zan-
Zhi ila Zahir Zephyrine Z=bL

popular pork is power to who wants bacon and razors

halleluja\
we want a song of glory\
now

and later for the tanks\
coming\
just over that hill

hal le lu *ya*\
i need myself to sing\
over this sweetly rising water\
death and endings always threatening\
our daily sun

59

will they finally set us naked against the tiger
will they strip us and lead us in to the colosseum
what little murders will they trick us into next
"kill him, he's an asshole"

all women

kept in droves, one little heifer allowed out at a time Jackie O or Marianne
Faithful, Cassandra, Briseis, to be be confused and go crazy to amuse the
warriors

Warsaw,

who named yu?

purposeful love

with the tide out the tall grey CIA sailors stay away.

here come the feet of the people
they are looking for a good time
cruel clowns
sit above them and mock them
the peoples' hunger makes these dolls divine
the clowns fall off the towers and trees like plums at the end of summer
purposeful love ploughs them under

Berkeley, California

climbing dream mountain
steep and high
where intelligent lizards
greet yu
and that sensual
dog

and that handsome angel up again
                              hovering on the blue
                                        just eight feet away

he has no feet
and extends
a draped dish
towards yu

                    yu turn away
                    and look far down

                         and see

                    far far below / sinister blue houses where
                    from gullet-shaped windows piano music
                    rises / played ever so lightly / by gigantic
                    professors of napalm

even from here
yu fear
to catch their eye

or to face the angel

in praise of bad things

praise milfoil weed, long green strands snagging the motors of powerboat;
praise man-eating grizzly bears and up-tight Iranians; praise rust, mold,
moths, racoons, buzzards, housemice, sharks; everything that breaks us
down and cleans up the mess and drives us on to think and plan and turn
ourselves about

praise the *hawk* that steals the *heron's* fish; praise the *heron* raising her
true harsh cry of protest; praise the biker gang of local *crows* and the
seven angelic screaming *gulls* that wheel about together at last calling:

drop it
drop it
drop it

and the *humans* on the shore
praise them
that call out

> *yay gulls*
> *yay crows*
> *go go go go*
> *hawk*
> *go*

it

when i go for it
it
ducks and dives and answers
not my need
but my hunger
from a false distance like a movie

suddenly it's not land i'm walking on my usual feet in leaky boots
sinking into the forest bog

but the palm of its hand
and it does not love me
does not love me

so i
must go for it
go for it again
for an answer
compatible
with my humanity

before daybreak
in the black winter night
   it

      floods my house, smashes the windows and doors carries off
      my pots and cups and plates teapot, basin, pail, honey and
      jars of cereals and beans

a trunk full of clothes
a gallon jug half full!
my wine! my wine!

and leaves me
a clean floor

'spring moves fast now'

spring moves fast now
        Old Squaw Dick and Bufflehead, Scoter and Scaup, tribal birds
                are leaving
                            now we
                      are coming out
                  dumping gasoline
                on the green waters
            of heavenly eating
          emotoring roar
        of mechanical gorilla
      shriek and swing
    ancient slaves
au to mo tons
        cut off from everything
          but twined by our arts
            in a cord that comes
            out of mind
            and winds
           round yr neck
           jerks
         back yr jaw
             muffs
         yr bite
yu
    hang on
        with yr teeth
            yr lips and tongue
            to yr neighbour

                        dream world
                          i have a canoe
                            to enter you
        the shimmering dish

65

                    on which the fish
                    eat and are eaten

earth's glass armour
for her tilt
with the sun

                              satin
                                   easy chair
                                        for gulls
                         flasher
                         sinker
                         line
                         and
                         hook
                         to me
                         eyeball
                    of this poet planet
                         ocean sea

                         source
                         of heron's
                         sacred
                    self absorption

April for Z

1

cantankerous, a
razorfrill
of oystershell
danger for meat
a deal

old
incidental
friends
a recent
pleasure

bad
words
good

in
place
in
time

passion
gone
no
need

let
the goddess
speak

amusement
cruel
in Spring
from Mexico
male hummingbird
comes
two thousand miles
for
red
flowers
for
food
for
flight
for
red
flowers
for
food
for
fight
for
red
flowers
for
food
for
females
falling
on
him
from

                    the
                    sky
                        for
                            red
                        flowers
                    for
                        food
                for
            offspring
        he shall   never see

                    and for us
                    he will
                    not
                    see
                may he never know
the burden we've given him
        futility

                                but
                                we
                                now
                                up and down
                                towers

        trip   sun
                with the

some of the celebrations

april 8

which was the first day of Passover and the day before
Good Friday
some friends come by
Martha Miller and
Freya Circe
with a bottle of wine to
celebrate Martha Miller's
birthday

and i remember
Anna Perenna
the drinking goddess
reeling in the year

we
want

four cups of wine
for
Passover

we
have

hummingbirds
seafire
and water tribes gliding in

april 12

Easter Monday

fourth
day of Passover

Anna Perenna and some friends drop thru
red currant bushes
twittering
ah
ha
courant rouge
deadly red tide
or the flow of our blood
or the thunder of red shoes
running on the roof of the world

a temple for Parasvati

then i woke in a dream of rage
of a white-haired naked child
the blaze of her rage
the urge
of every being
        to be free

                        to rise
                            only
                    when the call comes

                                        hi
                                        we have
                                        a ring
                                        for you
                                        a fish
                                        to fly after
                                        buckwheat
                                        to sow

                    flutes
                    to play
                    in the bee

                                        gardeen

                    a temple
                    for Sarasvati

                    and the bomb
                        will be laid
                            in a sealed
                                tomb

monkey

(a game for a raid of babies)

here they are "up" the raiding bees come to destroy silence, the collective
accomplishment (radioactive voices) shrill commands of the unrestricted
ego trial of good nature, dirt poor, rich in excrement, billowing with
self importance, basting the roasting nerves of old liars with turtle juice
pending death, pending the overflow of rivers, the upending of this hand
made table, following third hand the expostulations of Aleister Crowley,
go up mountains, descend through waves, welcome back the tribes, ducks
and terns and loons, following the sun down every night, pursue the heat
of fallen bodies, chop, saw, scrape, sweat, descry the villains that want to
end this cacophony, nuclear, physicists and their childish cries of joy at
yet a new isotope, my own neutrons and protons held suspended over the
earth like a cloud with no rain but holding back the glad sun

undulant

the slow breezes with webs of exotic-seeming spiders that stalk over the
sea making a network of irritations and genuine inquiries, a new story
that the huge bored ear demands, new sexual stimulants,

a motivation to make a banquet — peace? the drumming of the mine
machinery and the book bindery robot metal jaws consuming that *we* may
consume the vengeance of the mother, enraged

that her life
not destroy other life; are the
leviathans about still
or have we scraped off this glowing pearl, the earth the last slimy trace of
    life?
do you deny how the waitress hates the meal, the dark predawn rising
    every day, servant of the lord?

and the lady?

the lady's days are gone in May

says June
hi, Julie, pass the spirits,
August sez, turn about, Septima
and Octavia sez, let's free people, Nina

Nina replies

no
and the unnamed
eleventh hour of each year
cries
all of poetry*
eh, Dee?*

and the doe
leaps over the holly bush in snow
January and February March on
with book and gun
and April

May
come

KEY?
KEY?
MON?
KEY?

for Dionysus

the spilling of the wine to Diana, diva, day goddess and sister of Zeus
who was so jealous that he used his anger unwisely and let his strength
multiply till all the beauty of the sea became airplanes, red jets today
streaking below the clouds over the low mountains of the islands, saying,
we are here, we celebrate our power, the force of the rich and the mighty,
a young god

may he lay soon under the mouths of a proud mistress may he be among
the multitudes of the unemployed, may she have bucks to keep him gently
stoned and laid back, let all the force fall this way to virgins and spinsters
of rhyme, typists and nurses, store clerks, models, social workers, wives
and whores, all women with a will for the end of the war as he blew it, for
life, peace,
love as under
the law
the fulfilment of hunger
frantic breaking of the black earth now
       in buds
          up

                  bullshit sez the blue god
                       off
              yr feel mind on yr slimy sooey
pig kiss sing laugh fall fall
make yr piece becoz yu come now where yu will or no
no no no no no no no no no no no no no no no no no no no no no no no
no no no no no no no no no no no no no no no no no no no no no no no

yu call

i will not

but

butterballs turn under
sweet split hairy

give in?
give in?
give in?

for the times there are no ones

1

yu said, "i cld see by her outfit that she was a cowgirl." as if blue sky chaps with golden suns cld be a whole new universe. deny the maw, they called us "ma", bear mother / the fixed trap / a well to trip into. John Barleycorn, cut off at the knee. free of the dreadful return. you need never come back. better yu don't he said with a steel eye. walk down the street and he returns to his secret cunts. let me sit on the edge of the marble cornice over the street. faces of devas and devis masked in rice powder as a carpet below. gardenias. silver leaf on. rose-water sherbet, the blue sky outside the white archway. black eyes glitter with malicious amusement. "taste!" and all the walls smash up at me.

living alone and liking it. the orange buoy out on the cove. a ship under trees under sail, surprised, like the ballerina finds she can leap. the czar is pleased, strokes his double pointed red beard. the king must die. every druid knows that.

i pick up yr voice thru yr poetry book. it's cheaper than c.b. what's more you don't have to have a p.a. and that's o.k.

i lost the map of the Sechelt peninsula at the Kam Gok Yuen restaurant.
i went back. it was gone. you who picked it up, i hope you got there, you
which are all and wander in these hard times till you find yr own. will
this help?

for the times there are no ones, puppet governments, palette knives
making mandarins for sure. "just give him that little twist of kindness."
lariats in the Old Long Chance. sapphire-eyed cow sky, El Rancho Verde,
green or true, de veras, palace of *el presidente* of Nicaragua, stuttering
slaves of self-made oil-in-can king. parrots walking about mocking the
silver servants, hushed terror of when yu fall-to-please. mad laughter.
apocalypse now, please. behold the Zodiac and its motor.

i want i want i want i want and *i kill* all i cannot have. the sorrow of the
Kwakiutl chief. his release to go out to grief and God. and god help who
falls in his way. hence the sweet brother bearing doves and the blazing
heart of Jesus.

i decree silence. i decree all unnecessary motors die. i will listen to all
tales. no one will suspect i am deep in cosmic sleep. prescriptions for all
ills will drop out of my ears. no one will be saved.

Helen at the hearth holding the red-hot poker. volcanoes surround her
making vulgar noises. fat pots of bean-mud for the lost armies. the swan
flies by. she, the new wife, looks up. a crow drops sandals of bat-wings,
ants file by in the millions, each bearing a crumb of bread. blood will not
come, only ichor, she dreams, golden ichor, streaming upward from the
vagina like a cloud of gnats, a veil of freedom.

Black night and the white legs of Helen.

Cadillac, black as a sea of oil abandoned at full noon at the edge of the desert. the slave prince, draped in magenta, bows under the weight of the baby moles. i will find you a garden, he promises. supplication his own fountain. a captive most — tenderly taught. when you surrendered yr will yu began a dream path, fulfilled yr own predictions, stabbed the editor with a gilded parasol, baited traps for navigators, rivers ran out, seas ran dry, you are run by a new hormone. when yr foot falls it divides into five. but you forget the political divisions, the new duties. you are up to yr neck in invisibility. all you have to fear now is the fear of all. cut-off talking head.

specialists join the commissars. Saint Stalin smiles and embraces the
Beloved Comrade. everyone is glad. we have all got through this together.
much of what is precious to us we have kept. we live in terror of what we
have killed. ghosts stalk the Kremlin. we wonder if it is the janitor but the
place is kept so warm.

"what about the cabbage soup?" it is no longer real. the foreign
ambassadors can't stand the smell of it. the drains are poor. sometimes
i think, though, they break into the secret tunnels. think of the golden
treasures there. in fathoms of piss and shit. or suddenly purified by
methane explosions. soon there will be a subway. "I don't want a subway."
but comrade, everyone wants to come here and see you.

the small boats fly in, swerve, and fly out. the sun is speaking with the
cliffs. i will go out and listen.

the insects will not stay still. chainsaws scream at the trees. a brass band
marches through the graveyard and tramples down the waist high wheat.

at five p.m. every householder comes to the door and shoots a rifle. Boom
boom boom boom boom boom boom boom boom boom boom boom.

a half empty oil barrel is rolled onto the fire. in the golden meadow every
five minutes a small plane roars down. a five-year-old girl with a new
knife from her uncle cuts into a cat.

in a yellow robe i fly out of my cave distributing Chinese herbs, aconite,
cannabis, conium maculatum, homegrown cocaine. take *thisssssss take
thisssss i hissss* it will save you an eternity of grief. remember to rise high
as yu twist.

the burns of eternity are regarded with a snake's eye. my body writhes
in a script the elect read greedily.

what do i say?
what do i say?

hey chant pæans for old mermaids. they shout *woop. wow. hey.* they cry
ow. no. o. they crouch on the ground and cuddle their loved one, the
   river.
hoopo they howl and hit the brass gong for fifty dollars.

Max! Max! come out! call the cowgirls. is that a noose the foremost red

head holds or a silver girdle?
burn it! burn it!
the one like a horse!

shards of amber tortoise shell shoot from the horizon. the world egg is
recovering. through the cracks serpents fall then flower out into fire maps
of new continents. i can see where i must go but have no wheels.

the Prince of Starvation College, madam. at your service in every way.
forget cold destiny. i offer the most lubricious despotism. here, here touch
my sword.
this is how all age comes to flower. i bow humbly to yr cunt. i am yr meat.
i bring three hundred and sixty-five goblins to make each day madder
than the next. here is my jacket of boils and rubies. here is my sweet bland
breast. here my immaculate asshole for your consideration. my plumlike
scrotum, penis thick as a stump. forget the scrofula, it comes and goes
with the consideration of kings. my tongue! madam, my finger!

a fall of tinsel immediately enfolds him. a harpy shrieks and carries him
away. my right forearm has become jewelled enamel, three shades of
green: olive, emerald and jade. i think it hurts.

81

a delegation of five hundred children, comrade. they beg you to cease this crap. "let the little darlings in. give them books and roses and batteries and pulleys and awls and saws and hammers and chisels and screw drivers and squares. let them have transparent drums and saxophones of human bone, pianos of frozen formaldehyde, guitars of radium blue. quick, where are the monkeys to teach them language and red parrots for lovely laughter and lions to lick them clean."

it's all right, they say. we'd rather stay out here in the woods. don't worry about us taking over the meadows and streams. they say: back off, buddy, but please send out twenty gallons of yogurt, some honey and nuts. thanks.

silently, all night, schools fall like shrouds and they wake up facing a blackboard covered with rules that grow before their very eyes.

silence.
neither princesses nor princes shall wear crowns nor any jewel.
perfection is expected.
perfection looks like death but does not stink
nor grow vile roses. penetrate this at your peril.
essence engendereth permission.
sin not nor know what sin is.
bring this back multiplied a thousandfold
tomorrow morning before nine a.m.

now
divide.

and everyone runs out.

we're poor. we haven't a penny. they must have raised us to kill us but why do they smile at us so charming and let us rest on the warm breast?

but this one, this one just hisses.

it's a steaming manhole in old New York. the worst way to die, some say. and some say a slow life, hiding everybody's eyes. the high black cliffs on either side. ahead the apple green sun full of magenta birds. no, those are yr mothers.

sad fetus eyes. "are those hullucinations or more lies?" who says this? the collective unconscious is a witch. do we take the plunge into a new medium? why leave Atlantis of the blue spires? there's always some traveller comes back to tell us tales. but the womb will be no more, no more. we must dare air.

lies. lies. i can lie here forever and never venture.

you're a frog now. yr only a fish. quick, kids, catch it and skin it alive. let it gasp with horrified eyes in the sunshine. watch the pretty jelly mist and crack. laugh. swift now, find the little throbbing heart before the knowing goes. no? so you lost it. that was cruel. that was unkind.

punishment, expiation, antiquities like the garrote and the alarm clock. a border of nightingales around a streaming mist. Pythagorus, wake up! It's time for the class.

"they keep on coming without permission. i no longer care for the circle
nor the square. bliss is mine and a spare pair of lime coloured shorts,
a free haircut if ever i want one an endless round of drinks with the
demigods and heroes. they make fun of me, i think. they never seem to
piss and the one with the soft red bosom and the orange eyes calls me,
'My Little Curlicue' and licks her huge purple lips."

salvation is in smaller hands than these / we will pick at yr liver till
yu weep fire / try to understand / yr lantern is so handy / and we
can't just hang yu / yll be well thumbed by us / no page of yr mind
will not be blessed with grease from some repast / coffee stains and
seeds of strawberries will add complications to yr plots / you will know
everything. and we will know nothing at all.

a deal?

that yellow headed woodpecker.

the dark wood.

the blondes

july 1981
as more childrens' corpses are
unearthed from Fraser valley
floor

two aging dragon ladies with nothing to fight about but a limp chicken

Oulm Khalsoum singing:
"A Gar *fak*, in insilah aaaaaaaaaaaaaaaaaaaaaaaaaaaaaaaaaaaaaaaaaaa
goniiiiiiiiiiiiiiiiiiiiiiiiiiiiiiiiiiiiiiiiiiiiiiiiiiiiiiiiiiiiiiiiiiiiiiiii

all i want is a huge darkness
        that all memory be gone
           all wrong

                gone
            and a darkness a

darkness
      no more dawn   that comes on anyway
                o god no sez god no
                   more
                     creation
             the face of darkness creases with gold
the laughter of darkness becomes a hall of fire
a heaving belly about to blow
stones into stars

                     a blond fading

into new smoke   the pale blue eyes
              open
           broken
             open
             and

a baby
           cries
           cries
           cries
for who floated away on the boat

she comes back with the Boy in Blue who says he's afraid to die
he'd never stay down in the exploding hold
"i'd be up so fast the top of the ship would blast off"

and i'd lend him my old silk chador
                    for parachute

                                        barren thing
                                        the news
                                        the ditch
                                        between the
                                        blueberry
                                        field and the
                                        cranberry bog

              the roar in the air
           they're up there

                    circling

homelite 250

<pre>
                          this
                    is the chain

        it's connected
                  to a spark
              bright violet
                     white
                 or blue

                                          and they all
                                          go dancing
                                          off to rock
                                          and roll on
                                          midsummer

the crows in the trees
go
                    caw
                    caw
could they be having
conversations about the belly dancer on the shore
shaking her golden buns?

is there life
    in hiding
        i ask

                                          the little
                                          crab under
                                          the rock

                    it
              comes out
          with all its little brother and sisters
</pre>

hissing

    piss off, Max

                      i
                      smile with terror
                      at its
                      cuteness

there must
be beauty
in this
invention

two views of the western journey

view 1

for Cathy Ford
on Mayne Island

they have gone their way West and forgotten to seek the centre
El Dorado

"*no*

one

knows

now"

sing the old clowns of golden town

so how do we know
the old ones know?

only

turn

turn

turn

ding dong

clatter of joan

she

calling down to where

a little rivulet rings thru

the daisies

there to sit and wash
her pretty little feet
i want her clothes!
calls the old woman
looking behind her, the girl leaps to her feet and is gone from the high
beach to her canoe
that she must untie and shoot down the precipice revealed
by the   sinking   tide

if she can keep afloat on the inner current *his* speed does not matter
he stands there and he laughs
from what we now call Saturna Island to "Kuyper" island, then to
    Sney-ny-mo she fled

and he came and he took her back   had the women nurse her back to
    health   then he hauled up a great log
broke
both her legs
crushed
her feet

Part of this poem is based on a story about O–Chew–Wan, a semidivine local crazy solitary warrior who tried to discourage the white settlers from encroaching on the Gulf Islands of Southwestern British Columbia in the 1800's. He wore an illuminated snake in his hair and could disappear into rock cliff faces. Nevertheless he was captured by the Royal Navy and hanged in Victoria.

Part is also retelling a story about Tzouhalem, a famous and violent man, a warrior of the Cowichan nation. He was so much feared that people didn't dare refuse him anything that he demanded, including giving him any woman he asked for and he asked for many. Ultimately, the story goes, he got his own on Kuyper Island, when a group of women killed him in front of all the people, stabbing him from behind, much judgment having been passed on his actions in previous years. Sney-ny-mo is now known as Nanaimo,which means "people of many names" or "confederation" in island Halkomen.

Central to the poem is what is reported as a Hopi legend that all the North American tribes have a responsibility to regularly return to the centre of the continent, which is the home of the Hopi nation, some say the El Dorado that the Spanish misunderstood so ruthlessly. The European dream of unification, one Christian empire was, of course, regularly acted upon, providing valuable blood and bone meal for the hungry fields of all the little fatherlands of mother Europa. Golden Town was the capital that any peasant longed for during feudalism, ravaged as they were by their own military.

view 2

for Empress Maria Teresa and
the queens of Europe
and my friend Ruth Claire
wherever they wander

but they have gone their way West
      and forgotten to seek
            the golden fountain
          set

                fire
            to the oil
              wells

                oh they are all so
                uncontrolled
                those sons of yours,
                madam
                alas, madam
          they obey me not

they have gone their way West
      running out of the Russian and British empires respectively
            met and mated and sneered at all those others
fleeing the Aistian Galindian Sidovinian Selian Semigallian Curonian
   Skalvian Latgallian Yatvingian
Nadrovian Haliczian Transcarpathian Herzegovinian Dacian Moecian
   Thrasian Erpican Illyrian
Avaro-Slavs
met at the Hogbutcher's house in Chicago and fled
North on the railway
          stepped out onto the summer plains
              gone northeast to Cold Lake

                              to Pierce Lake
                          to Lac des Isles
                  canoed down the Waterhen River
              a governess and a "gentleman's gentleman"

          and sitting on a rise, made a fire
              found themselves surrounded by red twilight
              and they speak of Galicia
                  how she had fled Lvov to Vilna, Vilna to America
                                                              to
here

                          now
                  how
                  beautiful it is
                  how
              cold the wind
will become in winter
          and wolves

perhaps we should go back to a city — or a village — or a town ...
                  and bow again to lords?
                          ah, lords
                      she smiles
                  and he looks afraid
she
sees his fear and thinks
                      now he will leave me here
                          in this wilderness
he
sees her fear and hates her
it is she that has lead him to this god forsaken place

they both look out

into the long twilight
           they do not see
           the myriad fires
        not so very far away

    but they breathe   the wild roses

the blue eyes

        (they have only brown eyes)
i thought they owed me another twenty-five dollars or so
        but couldn't find the paper
                    "we make the finest paper," she smiled
            a red-decked doll, blue black clouds on her head
"and the meals are excellent; whatever you can kill"

                the terror of those days
                blue eyes looking lost
                        icepicks
                        striking fear
                        into humans
cheap thrills

                    the nexus of glittering beings
            hovering in the dark
"patience" they call
                "we have come to take you away"

ah let me be here awhile, i weep on my green stump
            come be my guests
                i will listen to yr wisdom
                    please teach me all you know

a procession of sages marks a fish on the ground; poinsettias burst
from the earth
            people come up bearing banners
very fast long march

it can't be borne, i cry
    snivelling in my beer in the Waldorf
        captivated by the huge velvet orchids emerging under the tables
            all around a sea a jungle
                i must know quickly.   what
am I?

                butterfly or
                fish

dark purple harbour

        and the sea and the sea is so soft today is so soft
today a grape that swells a grape that swells filling up
yr mouth filling up yr mouth
           filling up yr mouth   filling yr mouth
                 yr throat
                 yr mouth
                 yr throat
                    filling
           a grape that swells
a grape that swells   a grape that swells
is so soft today   is so soft
and the sea   and the sea
pressing
against
yr heart

                    magister
                    yu kneel
                    wanting me gone
                    wanting me gone
        wanting to come   wanting   wanting me gone
                        wanting

                  magister
                  yu kneel
              wanting to come
              wanting to come

outside our room
the world waits
intending
to set us straight

for the IWA's Jack Munro upon betraying Solidarity

(mode:helpless rage)

pickup of the month club
maybe one welfare recipient to take home
a lottery
sweet flower of "the great unwashed"
a perfume so rich
yu will give it its own space to watch the white temples full of singing in
the wild woods

pterodactylic hymns of heron broods
trumpet of Old Squaw Duck over
salt chuck

how
get
this
hook   fish
catch

armadas of trawlers and trollers, draggers and hookers
angry
that dreams be confined
by one scheme
a dead man's dream

when a man is weak   he is ignored or exploited
by
other men
and a woman
what will she see

a big cock
unemployed
that withereth away
like the State never will

six hundred miles from the shore
Space Mother waits

we go out to her
trembling

i wld defend yu against the life yu have chosen

deep in the thicket
i drive a dead car   its silver streak
                                                stalled in silence

next:
    crow sorrow
            crow gossip
                    crow long tales
                        crow jokes
                            crow rhetoric
                                crow democracy
                                    crow lobbying
                                        crow counting
                                    crow conspiracy
                                crow complaining
                        crow brilliant minds
            crow wars
                out on the sea
        electric wires moan

trillions
        of
            tree
                leaves

click
        like
            small
                stones

at the very end of the road

falling
the silk
shawl
catches
on a nail
on the wall
hangs
like a lei

wild
clematis
on old
black
cedars

"Sombrio
Valley"
on the back
of the black
t-shirt

back
of the Omineca
river under
the Omineca
mountains
at the very end
of the road
Old Hogum

country canada

the taking of the apple

the green boys bound in

to the tent

and state

women are responsible for war

there are two women in the store

ten

seated

men

the highway

*(for the mad woman
in the attic)*

i was walking in white
where the ghost women had walked before me

i wanted to die
i wanted to take people with me

the lowlanders
how they had to go there

their brown cows
their ordinary green

backup to babylon

'stumbling along in paradise'

stumbling along in paradise the old loves cannot renew themselves
but must without the deepest most unimaginable sleep
the king of all creation sez now the bird cries
zap zap zap their egyptian songs call off the grand show
only for a club member the elephant will cry

cry now and lose this twentieth century vocabulary
it's not enough to whine
we need old time rioters to bring on the spring
forget the memory of betraying brothers' dope smoking honky friends
    whose only fertility is
perfect hate
and a slackness re adjectives

try to teach us what we're hot for
the old time liars need a new dream daily
it's always there
sometimes there is nothing

but are we reely dancing yet?

feb 84 francis street

i thot i wld wake with chinese singing coming out my eyes / i knew the
cat woman wld come and be gone / i knew the giant red horse wld leap
across vancouver harbour / there was no doubt in my mind my friends
wld take off in balloons to the rocky mountains there to find emeralds
everywhere

let's go, liquid of oceans / lets blend the marines of the globe into the
green jelly of our will / take yr naked sailors up the hill / come down
alone / cantaloup cheap in the bin / longtime downtown coalyards / give
children tape measures to take their share of the earth / give everyone
new hoes to turn every second street into a potato patch / no doubt flocks
of peacocks will live in the concrete towers; no doubt long dead queens
rise and sing for a bite of yr supper

but i never thot those kids could take jail / we were all primed for it / i
threw off my cap and collar and veil / threw the forms in triplicate to the
ground / then bent down and picked them up because i knew some old
servant would have to

longing for the summer river i took a job sweeping the jail house labyrinth
/ my neck is lumping / my wings hang in dead skin / but i am crooning
/ i am scrying / i am hanging in there for the sun dance / we will colour
this concrete the four sacred symbols of the universe / we will take the
magistrates naked to face the music / they will sing wildly with us / they
will tell us of lost days wandering / how imprisoned in foul gold, cut off
from mucous by ancient words / guards of steel / forced by ivory angels
to flow out at dawn to pour poison from the sky / to rise before their
dreamtime to sign death warrants / now my friends will free them / now
the judges will see / they will be happy to go on foot to the sea / seesaw
with strangers / clap / crippled / in the centre of the dance

tuesday

grieving the horror of the young blondes (blonds)
        and having to turn away
              from their beauty
                  as they
                      claw
                    toward the
                        sun
                      half way down
                into
                  the town

          just
                for a sip
                    of a look
                        at it

              red and rusty blue babylon
ballantyne pier

        copters
        carry
        vaults

                it was a bluegrey evening
yellow this morning

wednesday

once again
paper
boxes
on the back
steps

                              sunlight above
                                   but
                          rain on the hill below

many little men
hammering again
and a small voice cries
help

pecker

here's another big red ship come in
full of fatal friends

meet me just half way up the goddam mountain please
just half way up

or start at the bottom
peckerpeckerpeckerpeckerpeckerpeckerpeckerpeckerpeckerpeckerpeckerp
eckerpeckerpecker

go down to the water
                                        by Neptune sailing
                        by grain towers
                                celadon blue
by Ceres
                by shy whores

                                streetlit
                                        ladies' table

under
massy
mountains
thick green
hairs

                is
                        there
                                running
                                        azure
        interference?

109

right
now

i wanted to make a melody
speak of the wretched past
fresh snow
up
there

                         no
                            let's be foresworn
                              and forever
                                 parted

                                 the love
                                 that way
                               more true
                                   in
                               little bands
                               of angels

old gothic

when the daughters of the night
meet the children of the moon
it is useless to complain get out of my garden
the old folk come anyhow
to correct the lines yu have cut in the sidewalk

what is borne out is
friendship with bad animals, not one
but worships the sun

when the daughters of the night
meet the children of the moon
they are cued in by arrogant strangers
they don't pass up the chance to eat greasy fried
they look at yu through goldfish bowls
they perpetuate their species in ink

they spin on their sockets singing, "Monday Monday Monday"
they mass with the million starlings up and down the town
the inside city of string saying
"My cousin is Joy. Let's get over that rainbow.
Can we make of philosophy an iron fence, a zoo of generals?"

this silence i need is worse than dirt

the killer collapses on a bed of coals

it seems it's love i'm against and all
correct procedure

when the daughters of the night meet the children of day
they still want to run along the telephone wires through
the amethyst corridor of rain

a violinist is hanged from the weirdest of trees
the tallest and most chilling
on that abandoned table land
just under
the mountain beyond sleep

a thought of rivers

           it is these things i am long gone from

no
more
floa
ting

          hear
                   we are always here
tittering at yr knowing
         up in the leaves
lies
                  a warm animal
        longing
           . for yu
and grinning
            there is something

            yu don't know

caught at yet
another
trick
memory
i
point
like a trained
seal

on her nose
a globe
painted
red
white
yellow
blue

the japanese word i wrote down then lost the page
wabi sabi
the stripped branch of a clump of grapes
lying on
a styrofoam tray

roar of truck
up hill
hammers
bang

there are rivers running
in and under this

hill
ancestors have buried them

relief to the eyes
the old frame house
a weathered glow
of snow clouds

dead trucks
girdle the walls

one
bare
tree

technology

it's gone on
so
long
the fish
creel
the
detail

people with no space
people with time

when the machines can slow down;
to our pace
we're all doing o.k.

hunters
trained to laugh
at death
come to the city
to see

                          fools

      night workers   mad plumbers

                   the great
               silver
            crescent
         wrench
           swinging

              in the
                  sky

velvet

yu sed
velvet
yu grabbed it

      and yu *wouldn't* let it go

so my father

      maybe *now* yu sit drinking good wine
       with Colette in her mother's garden

      outside the walls
     the cat in the snow
          howls with desire
    for the birds on the boughs
     and the balconies
        for robins drunk on rotten berries
       for the dear old woman
         who can no longer hear

       it's a wise child knows
          what to let go

           some quiet place
with iguanas, please

'the way all poetry ends'

the way all poetry ends
sssssssssssssssssssssss

                                                 whispering

i will come again

there are cities
of refugees

                                                       white boxes
                                                       on
                                                       helium
                                                       blue

                             con
                          current
                          halos
                          of
                          scarlet
                          sickening
                          power

                          Helios

                                        how to speak

                                   the lizard might
                                        fix yu with
                                  its yellow eye

sainte

horned

       singer

             grows

                    quietly

                          there

                            is

                                no

                          practice

             railway track at the sea
                 is there a slaughtered beast that forgives?
              The Sloppy Dirty Drunkard Corporation

if art is the aim

          if jude is the end

                   hopeless

                                 saint

              sits in the back of
                the bus depot

the rest

the midnight train
        going on the cloud
                sequence
                      non
                  sequitur
                quitter
leave this space

silence

this
Stanislavsky
allows
        that the people sit
          in a huge hall
      and roar for the rose
            the
        inconsequential

    Lilith   Adonis

      ila–a–la–halla–a–

      indulgent
        to
           our
     needs

      a phrase
        to
    scoff

who?

we
smell
like clam sometime
the waters of Burrard inlet wash us with warm
Fraser river mud
and we sink
into our long
established
homey holes

worm
turn
in lovely
slime
soft and persistent
push
push
barrows for our souls'
worth

worm
dear friend
lets me know
tells me:
"worm"
says
"forget the horror
of infinity

who
of us
won't finally desire the dark
slipping

sliding
licking
gyring
hiding from
the terrible
sky?"

worm:
ur u bor us
who
we could not bear
to see

the fence

finally the system of life is green with fullgrown vine leaves
hushed and sweet

suddenly a tall man steps from behind the fence and seizes
a friend of mine, a Jewish woman and demands to know if she is
Christian

she is silent and he cuts the head off her body and throws it to the ground
we are frozen in this dream and he picks up the head and steals away
behind the fence

what

is it

           yr whispering to yrself

                                 about

the bang

                 on the ninth floor

                     balcony

                                       could be

                             that black cadillac

                                   in the alley

                                      below

                         glittering

                broken

           bottles

on the bulldozed

                garden

                         pussywillows

                         and

                         pink

mist

                starling

           sings

                    as any bird can

in city

            whistles and shrieks

                                   i was born

                                   in this horn

                    singing

        this

artifice

elegy for Challenger

strontium
ium
iiiiiiiiiiiiiiiiiiiiiiiiiiiiiiiiiiiiiiiiiiiiiiiiiiiiiiiiiiiiiiiiiiiiiiiiiiiiiiiiiiiiiiiiiiiiiiiiiiiiiiii
      uuuuuuuuuuuuuuuuuuuuuuuuuuuuuuuuuuuuuuuuuuuuuuuuuuuuuuuu
        mmmmmmmmmmmmmmmmmmmmmmmmmmmmmm

ivory
narwhal
walrus
mammoth

ebony
ivory
dice, billiard balls, piano keys, teeth

ivy
      "climbing evergreen shrub, with dark-green shining leaves"
            five angled
              ixia
          ixion's wheel

         "izard, capriform antelope of the Pyrenees
          allied to chamois"

art

the old king of the right
makes music mindlessly
his flute the bone
of some alien limb

he enters in a cloud
of soft steel clash

stops
centred
like a shard

then a slow walk through forsythia

there is the fast dance
of a school of fools

and a bad creature
on the sidelines
pondering

Iranian raptures

                    snooker
                    comes
    coloured balls   all over peas
                    sign
                    sym
                    bolled

                                        fathers
                                        all gathered
                                        in brown
                                        halls

                    little
                    fathers

                    bees
part of god's great dream
of warts
and greens

round

peace for the children of pirates
                  peace for the children of pirates
                                    peace for the children of pirates
dead in the night
                  dead in the night
                                    dead in the night
nothing
                  nothing
                                    nothing
porridge and peas
                  porridge and peas
                                    porridge and peas
yellow seas
                  yellow seas
                                    yellow seas
elephants participate
                  elephants participate
                                    elephants participate
go where i send you
                  go where i send you
                                    go where i send you
the next bed will be green
                  the next bed will be green
                                    the next bed will be green

whitewashing our manœuvrings

>   the goddess of those days
> wandering angels
>   agents of robin goodfellow
>   called "devil"
>   the face of Lenin
> like that of Ludwig the Mad
>   of Bavarian castles
>   of dark blue marble face down in the slime of the lake
>   drunk on a summer evening
>   after feasting on cock

>   so we go for control
>   that's
> clear

>   perish the pests
>   gnats, little flies, mosquitos, lice
>   come to tell you how
>   terrible

>   turquoise
>   dragonflies

>   that lady with the jade
>   fingernails

Loretta Lynn

tennessee mountain storm talking down to the guys and finding
just how much they understand you
the last verse in its beauty
garbled by the little cuban in the front row
who would at any price
please you

could be jive, could be come on
yeah
seize the house

carry me away just about to any lost ghost town in the Rockies
be scarried

it's the old
process
that's what i'm scab and long for

prurient gardens
with those perfectly round trees

age of ivory, of sunlight, of castrati

not "Angles" sed St. Pat
but "angels"

i had to buy a new broom

1

he has on a kilt of lemon leaves. the demon at the gate. at each hour some angel saying, "come." at each day. each minute. each second.

seasoned as to the meat the careful inquisition. lazy the goat's walk up the perfect road of marble. it's the confusion over the owl they are for. pour out your long ribbon of spine over pineland in summer heat. the beach is full of boat people. they are looking among the reeds. prone the kid screams.

2

continue with this ruby face. its eyes that are simply openings into the public sky. pedal the boat. there's never any wind on this old oblong pool. pears on this tree in golden nowhere. i fled when i saw red skirts. the radio is irrelevant he thought he heard his master say part me a long park in all this rubble. first we have to search for the bodies. first. first is hurry up and forget yr socks. the volcano is erupting and we've got to run.

but the demon was lying and i have forgotten everything

yu will be lent
the cypher
as yu have been given
the glyph

fall far off now. the lean farmer comes to the fence. a battle ship
painted azure with yellow numbers

parliament is out shouts
september.
yu have to do orders, requisitions.
lions jump out the king's
back door. the desert never looked so good. it was radiant with radium.

3

peleponesia a subtle turn of asthma it's a kind of moral code green ducks
come up to fish yu
no more days.

i like the rules
less and less

here's a penny for yr dread
the kid with the collar was missing teeth   his mistress thot
he shld not have come so far   it was pretty well painted

out of the bowl of rice the duck's head emerged
there was dismay in the stands   the goddess kissed the referee
crucify her, crucify her   the red face of a Rooosevelt a Truman

they put it behind the bushes
we have forgotten

pick a pit of pickled petters   all wet at their picnic on the moon
pumas appear   and very grizzly bears
                                "hey! cut that fucking pounding out!"
the masks of McLuhan like

                                        the islets of Langerhans
                                        a coil not a serpent
                                            sez the sparrow
                                                i'm wise

prayer for an ancient merchant

place

                needle   horses

killing

bronze masks   colon   keel

decolonizing

                              too many s's

so yes to s's   something

seawracked   killing

author of fortune

           and stance

                          wooden disk

                                  gaudy border

           liliaceous

a pragmatist looks sternly at trees

        yu
can't write anything now
      yr friends are wanting to build a house
           but the land has been sold
               from under their feet
                   by The Great Lady
                       to buy some more Limoges

potters crofters websters fullers fletchers spinsters smiths
      a garland of old timers to replace
            the ghosts
limping out of "no auberge
that forest where many died
bleeding from their stumps
or blind"

                     the sirens of hell
                       howl
the demand for our love of humanity
    we face north
       and bow
          then we turn to each of the points of the rose
             which is our planet
             cool in the calyx
               under the ogling stare of
                 the sun

          i open my door to the sky
look up
       see
a huge eye

                 i
                 return to

                              being
                              minute
                              molecular
                              and
                              not a little electronic

and the planes
BOOMMMMMMMMMMMMMMMMMMMMMMMmmmmmmmmm
mmmmmmmmmmmmmmmmmmmmmmmmmmmmmmmmmmmm
mmmmmmmmmmmmmmmmmmmmmmmmmmmmmmmmmmmm
mmmmmmmmmmmmmmmmmmmmmmmmmmmmmmmmmmmm
mmmmmmmmmmmmmmmmmMMMMMMMMMMMMMMMMMMM
MMMMMMMMMMMMMMMMMMMMMMMMMMMMMMMMMMMM
MMMMMMMMMMMMMMMMMMMMMMMMMMMMMMMMMMMM
MMMMMMMMMMMMMMMMMMMMMMMMMMMMMMMMMMMM

I'mmmmmmmmmmmmmmmmmmmmmmmmmmmmmmmmmmmmm
hiding inside
saying
i have no wish to be Indira or Mengele
                    Margaret or Marguerite or
                            Mary or Martha; not Marta the Martyr
meeting the mitre

                    may
          maybe
                    or
Marsha
               old musical friend
                            fluting
                            floating
                            fingers
                    of the "flouting world"
                            that wild garden where

                              136

                    between the taverns and the
                         vineyards

hopyards
next to
junk
yards

alba for Howard

july 14, 1986; march 12, 1993

hyssop and rue
the moon
inconjunct
void-of-course
my mouth
stuffed with dust
i go rowing with Charon

these
are
funeral games

this
is
a tragic
race

this
is
a word game
a world game
sweet flood of hate
smile of fire
bones
immolate

trees
cannot save themselves
from worm or butterfly
entire species die
in this coarse course

soothed
with reason
in summer
the sweet brief place

i write this at dawn
when there is
song

notes for an opera for Chinatown

fall 85, spring 86

is where the walls are
                    where you are?

Old Homogenous
            digs away
                    at the Inner City
                        with his huge toy
                                the orange back hoe

                                        antique
                                            tiles
                                        in the garden
                                        shattered
                                        today

yes they hang in a show
those things that go on
in the shadows

there is nothing elegant
in this city
but our mothers

they have cropped their black hair
it lies in mounds
at the end of unlighted corridors

i give myself salt
i think they are all heroes
there is gibbering, gibbering

the god comes, draped, ancient
smiles without a word, passes
into the dusty alley

140

the blue eye of television
eats all shadow

it reaches from its box
cuts my eyelids off

telling me everything
i didn't want to need to know

the madman
tangles with the girl in the alley

the mothers in red shoes
run along erecting walls

that are spells
     that long ago
          held them in hell
               amongst blue flowers
                    where the yellow light of autumn fell
and fishlike twisting in the green darkness
          flew to the tower and sang
               something is come
                    talk to the daemon in the alley who sez
i will serve you thoughts
     sizzling on the thick spectacles of Jean-Paul Sartre
          you will bow to the town
               with your amazing powers
             only bring the walls down!

even now the old man is pissing in pain
onto old tiles
and into a porcelain bowl
on a dais rimmed with brass

weeping that the woman died
      could not bear life without light
            went out stamping into the flashing traffic
shrieked with glee at the car that crashed her
      spinning through yellow asters
         into a sky
        that was green   of an unknown planet
          wanting azure
            the high sky of the ancient plain
              where her children starved
to feed them she fled
to the inner city

the god led her to a warehouse
the grey light hummed

    along the alley
        on top of all the walls
          stood beautiful wisemen
           dressed in red
             paper
under the darkened arch she tottered
ranting the names of her great grand daughters

       a thousand white wings
      a storming sea of terror
    and a stench to end all breathing

the madman hands her an axe
here is food he sez

she
          sees
                    a salmon coloured sea
many blue shoes
                              the garden of coriander, parsley and chives
garnish for this delight
               yellow melon flower
                         bak choi lo bak
a young man
          his shirt open
                    showing his breast
singing to the old men
               on strange
                         machines

the blood
spurting

                                                  scarlet
                                                  runners
                                                  on the
                                                  hard
                                                  blue sky

                                   madmen
                         on horses
               swinging axes
at the necks
          of children
               and women
                    shrieking
                         like chickens
                              and geese

an orderly	procession	of men	in black
an orderly	procession	of men	in black
an orderly	procession	of men	in black
an orderly	procession	of men	in black

the dancer's song

slugbread
a bird in fire
barbary bangles
a kid in the loft
under the last
roof
thieves' trains in pieces
parch me, peach, am i
corn to be crowned
with trees from the sea?
soon will rise swans
jungles have packed their luggage
and we will meet in the fat lady's field
under the fairground

Bagwan Dorff
is tinkering singing minds
into a pyre
fit for a fir
case in point
the body in a box

both
loves
land
from the satellite over Egypt

marshmallow candies
cap the raisin debt

girls and boys come out to play
ring the raddled roundelay
peal the palling din of day

a drone
of B-52s

                                sing a song of sirens
                           a pocketful of pylons
                     imported for siege
              for sinking imprisonments
        moral mirror making morals die
    mask of rainbow coloured hate
what u raise ur deer ones to be blind to

          in the inner court of light
             the bloom
                poem
                    try
          fall
      off
   this
line

               make hay
           after harvest
        the children
     work
   in the camp
do they know the waves are their mothers?
Mengele every technician pouring oil onto troubled waters
      making rubber

ducks

      swans

          mice

             of plastic ivory

               salut savon!

         once again the well-scrubbed hero
       bursts out of bubbles
    the house leaps up in an explosion from heaven
  the angels catch the pieces
      test
   skin prints for identities
write it all down

Acknowledgments

This is a book of ancient history, ravings, folly and struggle. The person I have turned into is not the woman in 1984, pictured by Elaine Brière. I still claim the poet's right of altering the orthography demanded of us in Grade School. So the format here is of resistance and surrender and resistance and . . . the fool's attempt to re-enter "The Garden." Nightmares and the beautiful terrible white page where voices are laid down.

Acknowledgments go to Rolf Maurer who worked hard on accepting the "tude" in the spelling, read carefully and found some obvious mistakes, and is responsible for the concrete in some of the pages. Of course, as publisher he gets credit and credit goes to Carellin Brooks for helping produce a respectably hefty publication. Thanks and acknowledgments go to Mona Fertig and Peter Haase of M(other)Tongue Press, Salt Spring Island, who produced the hand-craft book *Fire in the Cove* (2001) which contains many of these poems.

And before that Daphne Marlatt and Ingrid Klassen who put out the 1982 Coach House Press selected *Lost Language* and included some of these poems.

I also thank the many human beings that have kept me alive.

Maxine Gadd

Other New Star poetry titles

EXERCISES IN LIP POINTING   Annharte
ISBN 0-921586-92-2 $18 CDN | $16 US

ANARCHIVE   Stephen Collis
ISBN 1-55420-018-0 $18 CDN | $16 US

MINE   Stephen Collis
ISBN 0-921586-87-6 $18 CDN | $16 US

HAMMERTOWN   Peter Culley
ISBN 1-55420-000-8 $16 CDN | $16 US

WRITING CLASS: THE KOOTENAY SCHOOL OF WRITING ANTHOLOGY
Andrew Klobucar & Michael Barnholden, eds.
ISBN 0-921586-68-x $21 CDN | $20 US

LIGATURES   Donato Mancini
ISBN 1-55420-017-2 $18 CDN | $16 US

THE WEATHER   Lisa Robertson
ISBN 0-921586-81-7 $16 CDN | $16 US

DEBBIE: AN EPIC   Lisa Robertson
ISBN 0-921586-61-2 $16 CDN | $16 US

XECLOGUE   Lisa Robertson
ISBN 0-921586-72-8 $16 CDN | $16 US

SILT   Jordan Scott
ISBN 1-55420-012-1 $16 CDN | $16 US

AT ANDY'S   George Stanley
ISBN 0-921586-76-0 $16 CDN | $16 US

GENTLE NORTHERN SUMMER   George Stanley
ISBN 0-921586-54-x $16 CDN | $16 US